radiogenesis

poems 1986 — 2006

by
thomas rain crowe

Introduction by Jack Hirschman

MAIN STREET RAG PUBLISHING COMPANY
CHARLOTTE, NORTH CAROLINA

Copyright © 2007 Thomas Rain Crowe
Author photo by Kenn Long
Cover image by Randy Mayes, courtesy of iStock.com

Acknowledgments

Some of the poems in this volume first appeared in the following publications:

Nexus, cold drill, Split City, BullHead, POINT, Argus (Ireland), *The Naked Fundamentalist, Pine Mountain Sand & Gravel, Lonzies Fried Chicken, North River Review, The Invisible Academy, Out 'N About, The Cuirt Journal* (Ireland), *Now & Then, The Café Review, Oyster Boy Review, Poems & Plays, Main Street Journal* (England), *Puente* (Scotland), *NorthWords* (Scotland), *Rapid River Review, WP Journal* (Ireland), *First Edition* (Ireland), *Fife Lines* (Scotland), *Black Mountain Review* (Ireland), *Melting Trees Review, Reflections, drift, SideShow, Milestones, 5 AM, Stalker* (France), *Triages* (France), *THE SHOp* (Ireland), *Passages North, Nantahala Review, Main Street Rag, Poems Niederngasse* (Switzerland), *Chimera* (England), *StrangeRoad*.

"Hard Work" first appeared as part of a Holocene recording in 1991 entitled *The Sound of Light* with accompaniment by musicians Eugene Friesen and Paul Sullivan.

"Iris" was part of a short run limited edition printing of a chapbook of the same name by New Native Press in 1992.

Library of Congress Control Number: 2007931152

ISBN 13: 978-1-59948-082-4
ISBN 10: 1-59948-082-4

Produced in the United States of America

Main Street Rag
P.O. Box 690100
Charlotte, NC 28227
www.MainStreetRag.com

*for Ken Wainio (1952-2006), Michael Davitt (1950-2005)
and Sam Gray (1940-2005) in memory
and for all my teachers*

Contents

Introduction by Jack Hirschman. vii
Radiogenesis 1

NIGHT VISION

Hard Work 5
Moondrunk 6
Flood 8
Night Vision. 10
Narrenturm 12
The King of Bells 13
Say the Unspoken Word 15
Oeillade. 17
Those Who Are Lucky in Love 18
Palimpsest 19
Cantilever 21
Poem for Sylvia Plath 22
The Flowers 24
There Are No Snakes in Ireland 25
Iris 26
Translation 27
Homelands 28
Breast Feeding 29
What We Do 30
Mood Swings 32
Fame 33
Cenotaph 35
Ambition 36
Seduction 37
Bringing Down the House 38
After a Quarrel 39
Black Butterflies 40
What She Said 42
Writing 43

THE CALLIGRAPHY OF FIRE

Modern 47
Learning Latin 48
Middle Class 49
The Calligraphy of Fire 50
Frozen Music 51
Oracle 52
Somebody 53
Mythology 54
Sour Candy 55
When the White Light 56
With Deep Breeze Slow on Air 57
Long Lines 58
Knowledge 59
Estates 60
On the Wee White Rock 61
By White Road and Thistle 63
Voice 64
Newgrange 65
The Wild Ducks at Coole 66
Evensong 67
The Florescent Eye 69
The Big Here/The Long Now 70
Io 72
Machu Picchu 73
What Would the Would-be Wise 74
The Alma Mater of a Kiss 75
Immortality 76
Not Even in the Nil of Night 77
Where the White Waves 78
Meetings 79

About the Author
Other Titles

An Introduction

When I first met Thomas Rain Crowe, in the North Beach section of San Francisco in the mid-seventies, he was a young poet who had come from the Carolinas fueled by images of the Beat generation in that city. I got to know him rather well in the cafes of North Beach. Though he was from rural North Carolina, he revealed sophistication with respect to poetry that even some of the more urban and urbane young poets of those days lacked. For one thing, he had an intuitive sense of the class struggle, and in what is perhaps his most memorable poem of that period, "I Wash Your Dishes, America," he reveals a strong sense of justice with respect to workers oppressed in their jobs, their wages, and at a time of the war and post-war Vietnam days. In another respect as well, Tom was, like myself, involved with the cultural arsenal of translating other poets. He understood, as many of the "Beat opportunists" would not, that the translation of poets from other countries was an important part of street activity; and when he edited an issue of the important street magazine, *Beatitude*, he made sure to add a number of translations, his own included, to give the street an international air. On another occasion he joined myself and Luke Breit on a journey to the maximum security section of Folsom Prison where he participated in a poetry workshop led by the Nicaraguan poet, Pancho Aguila.

It was during those years in North Beach that Tom also began to be influenced by surrealist notation. There were some poets on the Beach in those days who were influenced by Philip Lamantia, and Tom was aware of them; indeed he became friends with the likes of the late Ken Wainio. This surrealist element is important in understanding Crowe because, for example, in the very first line of the title and in effect dedicatory poem of this volume, "Radiogenesis," he writes:

The mind is a car radio. The body is Cocteau's Orpheus.

Anyone who has seen Cocteau's <u>Orphee</u>, that masterpiece of a film made a few years after the end of WW2, will know what Crowe is referencing: the car radio in the film pours out a surrealist poetry in what is one of the most visionary and inspiring mixed-media events in modern cinema. That scene has had a lasting influence on many poets and visual artists. I recall having many conversations with Wallace Berman—the brilliant foto-montagist and "Cocteau" of the hip scene in Los Angeles in the sixties and seventies, about that event.

The poetry that poured out of the radio was a cascade of metaphors and mysteries of the magic of metaphor.

In a way, *Radiogenesis* is an extension and refinement of that Cocteau event.

Because Crowe has cleared a lot of his youthful surrealist murkiness from his lines, he gives us here a series of what are in effect Orphic love poems. The figure of Eurydice is never far from the evoked feminine forms. But there is also this:

One of the dynamics of that radio event in the Cocteau film is that poetry strikes the sensibility as if it itself were received and in the service of some higher, even more mysterious, power. That is what textures the event with its particularly unique coloring.

In many of the poems in *Radiogenesis*, Crowe arrives at such texturing, even when he is clearly threading his lines, or grounding them, in more declarative and even philosophical yearnings.

And there is yet another aspect to this book that both reverberates with the Cocteau event and yet shows Crowe at his original best: in the Cocteau film, the words come from the radio with an immediacy and even an urgency in their invention. An aspect of that is received in such a manner because, with the development of modern technology, our sense of immediacy has been replaced—for better or worse—by the instrumentalities of our own invention. Thus, for many today, television is their real immediacy.

Thomas Rain Crowe

For Crowe, immediacy and urgency are manifested in an ample use of the imperative tense. In many poems, the individual or—even—the collective, reader, is urged to "do" something.

What?

Herein lies one of the delightful mysteries of this book.

The poet—in many of the poems—evokes the Kiss. Behind many of the imperatives he uses is the journey to the Kiss. Because this is above all a book of love poems.

The glorification of the woman and through her of the feminine depths of all things is the sea in which Crowe breast-strokes with both ease and anguish. And with no little of the magical realism that manifests as a romantic display. A line like *My body was made from the moisture on her mouth* is clearly a fusion of both orphic and biological vividness.

And it should not be overlooked that, throughout this book, there is a play on both surrealist and realist imagery. Crowe is not wired to some catalog of exquisite tropes of an "imagination-is-all" sloganing. He does indeed abandon himself to the lyrical metaphor, under the strong influence as well of Dylan Thomas, and to that alchemy of the Word that redounds to Rimbaud. But there is a strong realist tension in this book, and such realism gives the *sur* in surrealism a grounding drive toward love that provides the clearing that illuminates the paths of his imagery with the honest feelings that surrealism often shrinks from or covers up.

It is in that clearing that these poems most profoundly sing.

Jack Hirschman
San Francisco
August, 2006

RADIOGENESIS
poem for synthesizer & voice

The mind is a car radio. The body is Cocteau's Orpheus.
The sexual attraction is toward the car. The car as Delphic lover.
The love is for the radio, which is the spirit of the lover.
The love-act between radio and Poet is radiogenesis.
God is universal mind. Space-time is thought.
The radio is the mind. The mind of the Poet. The fertile egg.
The Poet whose dials are tuned to the right frequencies that
drink in cosmic milk. White knowledge.
Coming from the mind of God as sperm.
The union of sperm and fertile egg
creates the star-burst chemistry of genesis.
Radiogenesis.
The process of translation of these electrical impulses is genetic.
Electro-genetic. And the result is words.
The writing of these words makes the Poem.
Hours, at all hours, spent in the garage.
In the passenger's seat of the car. With the radio on.
Searching the dial for a voice on the other side of static.
For an inspired paradoxical juxtaposition of spoken sounds.
For a metaphor for daily life   as light.
Radiogenesis.
Or in attic rooms or dappleganged hotels listening
to the silence between screams for a sign of sanity.
Radiogenesis.
This is the Work. This is the stuff of a stuff better than sex.
The whore of Orpheus. The nightmare of Eurydice.
The thing invisible that becomes seen.
The King of the forgotten.
The siren Queen.

I.

NIGHT VISION

Tidy and cursed in my dove cooed room
I lie down thin and hear the good bells jaw—

—Dylan Thomas

HARD WORK

If there is anything against nature,
it is writing.
                        —*Carlos Fuentes*

It's like driving nails into the snow
to postpone the coming of spring.
The moon owning the mind like
the secret language of a laugh spoken by puppets who
pour knives into the trough of sleep.

Here, the prophecy of the past is
melting from the flames.
Drowning on air as if only water were
the oxygen of wind. In a life documented by drought.
This dying. This army of green nails sex-starved
for skin hurts like being stoned with the silence of
unfriendly eyes. And me with only some six-gun of ink.

Shots fired into the dark. Feet slipping through the ice.
Moon laughing as it disappears behind the giggles of daylight.
Arms dripping blood down onto the blank page of morning.
No sleep. Crows watching in the windows like peeping toms.
Nothing to eat. No thing soft nearby to
cuddle or kiss. Yet even with the lack of sunlight
this darkness   is born to us as poem.

MOONDRUNK

> *Where you've got nothing else construct ceremonies*
> *out of the air and breathe upon them.*
> —*Cormac McCarthy*, The Road

Drink the beautiful honey that
comes from the heart.
Even wine does not taste this good.
The girl who brings nectar to the boy in love
makes him want to kiss the sky.
He lingers forever near the bouquet of her breath.
Away from the wild trees.

Now go and kiss the moon.
Does this feel like your lover's lips?
Soon the pleasure will seep into the sacred glass.
And Isis will show up in a regalia of petals
and luminescent flesh.
Amidst this distraction
can you remember why you ran from the wind?
Or why the hole in the ocean was blue?
If the answer is yes, then for the moment
you are safe.
If the answer is no, then you are
out of luck.

Go back to the beginning and drink the wine
you didn't think was sweet.
And give the honey to the woman in your dreams.
Because this woman left you, this is like an
offering to the moon.
A cure for cyclones, forest fires, and drought.

If this doesn't make you drunk, then you
have more problems than can be cured with

radiogenesis

cheap paper and black ink.
Go forward and try and stand on
one leg or the carapace of a snail.
This should be easy. The snail is
in denial and doesn't believe that you exist.
Proving you are sober will be more difficult.
First you must send away for a dalliance through the mail.
Then you must wait for the moon to rise
from its daydream of the speed of light
before you are allowed to drink of
the antidote to wine—which is a lot like sex.
After reaching orgasm, try and get a good night's sleep.
But remember first to pray to the moon,
as it is lonely and close by
and demands praise.
To others this may sound like fun.
To the moon, ritual is like making love.
And it drinks us one by one.

FLOOD

Soon the river will be rolling over its banks.
Ask the rain how long water will come down.
All you'll get is secrets
not even a spy could break.

She says   trust the music and
the wind will set you free.
Believe it.
The dog is in its floating bed
and the rotting flowers are worshipping
the fever of a thousand fish
drinking blue champagne.

When the clouds explode in green fire
and sweet roses haunt the sad salt of cheeks,
what will become of the fiction of heart's desire?
What will starfuckers and homies say to the neutrinos in streets?

The river is rising.
I can tell from the pain in my chest.
The ducks and swans have migrated to another universe
and the adepts are all indoors   casting spells.
Think of this as the signature of Theos
or a postcard from Samothrace
that was sent in six hundred B.C.

The mystery is in the blood.
In the bloodletting of boats in the harbor.
Or the ritual of
setting the wedding cake on fire.

Even though your house is underwater,
think of this as good luck.
It could be worse.
The delirium tremens could have visited you
at a sacred ruin and the fireflies
turned into thirsty bats. Or the reflection of moonlight
become scorching heat from the sun!

Soon the rain will stop and
the fishermen will be as happy as mud.
You will sit there watching   and will know
when it's time for you to stay   or go.

radiogenesis

NIGHT VISION (SAMOTHRACE)

for Ken Wainio

> *Life's raw recruits go to the edge and over it because of the blinding immensity of what they do not know.*
> —Salman Rushdie

For ever I am led to oceans.
To blue worlds present with fish.
At night I breathe under water
in my dreams.
Every day is a mystery.
Each night   a gift offered in flesh to the gods.

When it rains, the water runs off my hair
in screams.
But I don't notice.
It's so loud here
that deafness is a lingua franca
and
peace of mind a cawing crow.
Always, there are the waves—

Amongst wild olives and aloe
the supplicants gaze at the moon.
Chanting mantras and feigning prayers
to a cult of cairns.

Near the end of Egypt, the donkey tracks
lead to the hot springs of Saos.
Where the goats and I go to bathe
and to escape the surreal spa of winter,
of snow on the sands.
If I were an apse in this place
maybe Isis would grant me a wish.

radiogenesis

A trip to the inner sanctum, or
the necropolis of torches that
is forbidden of feet.

Too often the terra cotta is scuttled
in my dump of a hotel   because the tourists
have gotten the best rooms.
But my spirit is undaunted,
and I take my torch and seek stoas
at midnight along the Aegean Sea.
My hair is still screaming.
The waves still coming in.
And even in darkness
I can see.

NARRENTURM

The things that unite us also break us apart.
Our own atoms colliding in the hit-and-run of space.
Whenever there is a kiss on the lips, it is always and
endlessly followed by a slap in the face. Terror
results from even the smallest history of pain.

Out on the battle lines what was once a word is
falling like a broken eggman from the wall. And

Faster than the speed-of-light is
only half fast enough to fashion a high-rise from grace.
From the 81st floor
only the lonely know how the soul
is dismembered by the rape of clocks. And
light at the end of a black hole is just a dream in
someone's mind at the crossroads of galaxies, jetlagged and forgotten,
    headed this way.

radiogenesis

THE KING OF BELLS

> *Because the earth survives beneath my feet,*
> *the pale god of my despair rejoices.*
>   —*Ali Ahmed Said*

Somewhere in the wind is
where I'll die.
Will fall down forever from
the lobotomy on Earth.
This world
with the frames of windows roaring
as a man roars in the final seconds before
the end of love.
You. You who want to reach nirvana
by kissing the shoe of Christ,
I have surrounded you with poems. What
is your next move, now?

When will we stop trading
machine-guns for rice?
Motherhood   for the price of pain —

Like the math of cities, Houston added to L.A.
is nothing. Added to Pittsburgh or Queens.
Still nothing. Zero is nothing. Nothing
near the shade of the sun.

Why not worship the rain?
When all sound of this century imitates language.
Like roses with psychic thorns.

I am crazed with the profound!
And I will die like lightning
in a flash!
My missing offspring will inherit
only words.

radiogenesis

Words that are passed on like the epiphany of seed as
stars.
A silent ringing. A chorus of a million mothers
remembering the best sex. Remembering the windsound of
clitoral thunder like a clarinet as it moans....

I will wait for the sounds of the ringing. Will wait forever
if forever is what it takes
until I am the 3rd of March and
everything made of velvet changes to Hell.
Until the end of daylight   or of smell.
I have lived for this silence.
I am the King of Bells!

radiogenesis

SAY THE UNSPOKEN WORD

I want to pray to gods that never heard of prayers.
—*Adonis*

Say the unspoken word
and
make me a memory
Take my name down from the marquee
Tell our mothers we're rich
and have gone off somewhere to fight
Have gone to town to sell our wings
Tired of the way love rubs wrong the music
and leaves dust
Rust of what was polished bronze before
it was buried in peat

Sing the lost chord or the last refrain of silence
and
move me to tears
Move me away from the burning fire
Tell those that have read my poems
that they were all written with stolen flames
Sunspots lifted from the mouths of saints
Baby's breath taken from the lips of burned books
Crooks climbing in windows for the Thief of Light

Think the last thought
and
remind me of music
Tell the songbirds fond of screens
we have run out of dimes
Riddled the life out of wombs
immaculate or chaste
in the convent of a smile
Where I have been locked up
in rooms of wind

radiogenesis

that blow like words do
in and after angry books of love unwritten
before I walked away.

OEILLADE

She said it with her eyes.
With lashes and lids in a single glance.
It was her six o'clock silence
that cut through doors and
windows that somehow took leave of my heart.
"Never marry a man who won't dance,"
she said, aiming a camera
at me like a hot poker, then
taking pictures of the noise.

There was nothing in me that she didn't like,
yet her passion perceived me as an empty room.
A lounge without chairs. An antechamber
without the rush of mirrors.

Whenever I opened my mouth,
apartheid fell out on the floor.
Prisoners of war or
the colors of fresh-cut grass—
It was the green she loved.
It had to be. There was nothing left
in the house to hock but air
coming in between boards in the wall
on a windy day.
"Love is this," she said.
"Like something sucking at our veins."

Today, there is sunshine, then
it rains.
The damn pursing of lips.
Feet that can't move to simple melody.
The silent screaming of her eyes.

radiogenesis

THOSE WHO ARE LUCKY IN LOVE
BRING THEIR OWN FATE TO THE DANCE

    Would you believe   that after a full day's work
        there would be something left
        for love?
    Kisses thrown on the fire.
        Or soft hands washing tired skin.

    In   heaven, it's the same as in this little house.
        A place to sleep, eat and
        make love after drinking too much wine.
    The   only difference—
        the kitchen, the lovers, and the
        animals outside are all in one bed.
        One room   with the obvious absence of clocks.

    Dark   dreams have shed light on this dance.
        Where feet and fear embrace
        the soles of the jig and the floor of every reel.
        These are not myths or the memories of angels,
        these are men and women dancing. They
    Bring covered dishes of raw meat
        to eat after the dance. They bring
        honey in ale to quench a flushed thirst.

    A little water goes a long way towards
        reviving the dead. Those who have
        died in spirit and cannot taste the
        honey in ale, or feel the fire in the dance.
    Light shines on their faces now that
        the sun has gone down and dusk
        lets go of their pain. And they are dancing.
        They are standing still.
        They have found a perfect stillness in the rain.

Thomas Rain Crowe

PALIMPSEST

From this oriel eyes swoon at the sight of
lovers who can't make their way to this page.
This page of washed out and washed again dreams.
This covering of turbid ink with
what was the elegiac thought of wind
wandering around in a pen so far from words.

How many times I've tried to write this poem!

Gravid of memory and ersatz of mind
I've gone to the well of wanting
to get this damn thing right!
But now I am keeping the company of cranes.
Rookeries of reason have become my perch
from where I look out over a losing world.

So I'll scratch out all the old vowels first,
then come back and whitewash all the *G*s.
Level all the *L*s and *P*s. Raze the *C*s and *D*s.
Snuff out the *V*s. Smother the *Q*s and *R*s.
Finish off the *T*s.

With what I've written gone to smithereens,
I'll begin the palingenesis of letters.
Become the troubleshooter, the tinder, of verbs.
The redeemer of mendable lines.

Whether with apostacy or empty thought,
I am backsliding ahead.
Maybe even ahead of my time
to get there first or last on this tottery ream.
Why try this again when so much failure has gone into
making this good?

radiogenesis

From my gargoyle's nest above the street,
I can see my words walking home after a hard day's work.
When they arrive, there will be nobody there.
There will be only vague cameras, lorgnettes,
zoom lenses and horned-rimmed quotations
to answer their questions and to cook their meals.

I don't mean to sound like a killjoy here,
but what else is there to think when outside
my windows they are building dungeons in the air?
And the only woman that wants to be my lover
is Cassandra, and she's beating down my door!
If nothing else I'll turn this wordy art into craft.
With bobbles and bangles, niellos and helixes
hanging from the edge of the page. I'll be all the rage!
In the end the naked rhymes will couple with
chaste rhythms that give birth to
syllabary that feigns life by putting on airs.
I know this sounds O so symbolic and stuffed shirt,
but what is a grandiloquent to do
in an age of chichi and frothy flash?

Enough of this conceit! Let's begin.
It's time for trucklings and sycophants to start
the toadeating, bootlicking, backscratching, ass-kissing,
mealymouthed, fawnery of helots, serfs and slaves.
In other words: put feather to the leaf. Be vainglorious
and narcissine to the point of being *de haut en bas*
if not sniffy and rude.
This is it!
My last chance.
So pick up the pen you word-ruck
and dance!

CANTILEVER

Only one end of a limb is
attached to the tree.
A sail used to lift up space.
An angle used to get your way.

Why pry into the business of the sky
using jargon that speaks in tongues?
Why put purchase to the task of a pinch bar,
or a winch to work as an iron crow
if the block and tackle only change the
course of the wind?

There is no hypocrisy in the sweet talk of night.
There is no charlatan in someone who spins a yarn.
There is no sham in the fudge of shoddy junk.
Only the doctored truth hung out to dry
like a namesake with all his baskets in one egg.

"Think ahead," she said, as we went out on a limb
to make love.
By the time the first act was over,
I already had a saw in my hands
and was sawing off flesh.

She likes this passion in me,
otherwise what would she be doing here
hanging around in the quiet trees?
There is no substitute for libido to this woman
who is only interested in my sex.
I'm hip to this scene, and so know my place.
And I'm there. Tree bound.
Planning my attack.
Armed only with wind's rhythms.
Watching her breach the distance
supported by that much wood.

POEM FOR SYLVIA PLATH WITHOUT EVEN LIGHTING THE STOVE

Even if the gas had been gone,
the heat from your eyes
would have been enough to
set the whole place on fire.
One-thousand-degree words
charred from the spark of space.

It was all in there—behind the iris.
Beyond the synapses of imagined pain.
Brown-eyed craters of moonlight
sun-starved from the food of love.
Even the *what-ifs* were not army enough
to stand against the dogs at the door.
The parade of children and husbands
standing in line. Waiting to get in.

If only Herodotus had known
the length of Medusa's hair. Or
the dark color of Jesus' blood.
The sweet taste of your own flesh,
something to help put on weight
after months of drinking   nothing but ink.

Where was the death mask that had been hidden
in the lantern of your face?
Or in the tinfoil baking carrots and
small potatoes in the stove—

No smoky veil or body part
can haul the ocean out of books.
They should have told you
there was no wine in this carafe!
No act of love in the sink.

Thomas Rain Crowe

radiogenesis

Bees are swarming in your memory,
now, decayed with grace.
Only prophets and bald boredom
are to blame.
The salty meat in the oven
is cooked and done.
Its juices, naked in our mouths,
taste sweet.

THE FLOWERS
after Dunblane

The news of tragedy travels fast.
Across water. Across barren land.
We have heard it, even here, in the pipes.
In the high-pitched wail of the wind.
And the echo of illusive poems.

When the tears have turned to stone
and there's no more murder left in our veins,
will the *we* in flowers bloom
finally from our children's beds?
Will the *am* in family recognize
its own seed, and come up willing
from the soil?

Death is the deal of dreams.
Unsavory, and
nothing but the bad-vibe of news
buried with those who have lived
long lives amidst flowers
and trees
not even the ghosts of these children will go near.
Each a flower on its own grave.

Good god, man, the guns!
What chance does a flower have
against weeds?

Sunrise, these days, looks more and more like night.
A black dawn afraid to get out
of its own bed.
Broken flowers in a broken crown.
Ashes, ashes, all fall down....

THERE ARE NO SNAKES IN IRELAND

"I can't think with an open door,"
she said, and after the door was shut
went on to say something about wind.
Wind in the source of wells.
In the beautiful vowels of a love with
no voice other than what eyes are
after tears, gone down cheeks
to a bridge where shock spans the violence
between suburbs and the history of sleep.
Rolls down like the water that runs downhill
to the Irish Sea
and under the thirteen bridges of Dublin,
by the breasts of Anna Livia Plurabelle
in stone. Runs like Bobbi Sands through a gap in
the hourglass of a hungry life. Runs like tears of censors
afraid of their own names. The names I had
for her, Anna Liffey, and have given you
now that the water is no longer as cold as neon,
as bright as love and light that sun shines on in the rain and
looks like you standing there on that bridge, St. Patrick,
who the pious say killed all the snakes in Ireland
even before the aftershock of ice
moved from County Cork to Kilkenny
like my lips across the tears of your poem-lost
face.

Dublin, Ireland
1997

IRIS
for Nan

Lips.
Lips, like the fever of
forget-me-nots wanting to be iris
and not wanting to
die at the end of spring, cover my sleep.
Cover me quilt-warm even as
the loss of you lingers like shy tears
behind this mask of being in love and the lover
who is listening for the sound of his own kiss.

Why must we wait for the rain
when we are already wet?
Already like lakewater caressing the earthy sex
of the shore.

Somewhere beneath the windrow of numbers we
have mowed and raked into time,
the dew is turning to heat.
Into a flower's wings
that want us to fly!

Here! Take the duende in Lorca's night like
the bouquet I have made for you wrapped up in poems.
This is why we are here. Is why I have built my own bed.
A vase for the sacred purple parts of you
I want to watch as you rest. My eyes making love to
every stem, leaf, and stamen in your dreams!

TRANSLATION

"I am leaving," she said.
It was more like code
than conversation.
More like sun talk than
anything that might have come from the moon.
Yet her face reflected in the night sun
was, for my eyes, too much light.
I just sat there
counting the letters in those three words
and I never got the same count twice.
It was either "she loves me,"
or "she loves me not."
Never seventeen, nineteen,
or twenty-three.

The next night as
I got ready for bed,
I heard the crickets through the window
out in the potato field
beyond the corn, counting.
After a hundred-and-sixty-three,
my numbers became letters.
The crickets' chirping became language
that was almost song.
I translated the letters, making words,
all night long.
In the morning, there was a note
in her hand on the kitchen table.
Five words born from darkness and
the mystery of unknown codes.
"I have changed my mind."

HOMELANDS

In the Marquesas, the villagers brought the
breadfruit and chickens down the mountain to
the rafts.
For more than a month the sailors
stayed afloat as an act of faith,
looking for land. For Hava Iki
which they called "Home."
Like those ancient travelers,
I set out on the raft of your body
sailing and drifting to find
a port-of-call.
Among the peaks of intense sacredness,
the silverswords stand out like the fingers
of my hands that have colonized your skin.
Have painted your lips the color of mirrors.
Have entered you
as the sky is pierced by a man in the moon each night.
After a thousand years, I am still digging
in the sand for clams. After a thousand more
only the middens will be left as a memory of food.
It is late at night
and in the moonlight I whisper your name.
"Weyeepi," I moan in the half light.
Either you are sleeping or
have left. Gone off on the rafts
of sailors and ghosts.
This is your land, and I am just
a white intruder here. An herbivore
in a land of meat, feeding on love.
How could the gods of emptiness even think
of letting you go?
Like a new native, I will be here forever.
A thousand miles from where I was born
and, like you, calling it "Home."

BREAST FEEDING

It may well have been Greece, there
that night in New York, with the rain
dripping onto her window ledge and
twilight covering the city like a golden shroud.
It was too late for dinner
even though the table was set and
the baby asleep in its bed.
The rain and the infant hunger growing
in my stomach, reminded me of childhood
in the southern mountains and how each summer
afternoon it stormed. And how calm it was
after the thunder and lightning had moved on.
After we made love and
after a long while, she said "I ache."
The warm milk from her large breasts
tasted like Greek honey
lying there by the window looking up
at the golden rain.

WHAT WE DO

Let what we love be what we do.
Be better than beauty or
the vibration of trees.
Be better than eyes
or what sees.
Take the hammer
from the one who drives nails
and start building arks.
Parks full of wolves.
Boats that are wormholes for bees
leaving the earth for the outback
of distant space.
For a land without race.

Let what we do be what we love.
Done down on the floor for
the sake of what we haven't dreamed.
Dreamed and fought for
in a millennium of silenced screams.
Screams louder than the laugh of
Joan of Arc playing with fire.
Of summer birds stranded in winter
perched up alone on apocalypse wire.
Higher than drugs dug deeper than
graves in the vein,
of the pain,
that is filling the air.

Let what we are know what we will be.
Know sex as the lover she is
singing to the square root of math.
Numb from numbers grown
too large for the sky.
Too crowded   for you.

radiogenesis

Too crowded   for I.
Why have we gone mad for the moon
with the sun in our eyes   and gone blind?
Gone kind   when the grin of money has teeth
sharpened and ready to bite.
Let's fight!

Let what we are be what we know.
Known for every deed we didn't do,
like words lifted from the page.
Famous for the lack of light   or rage
ending in nerves free-falling from
the grip of grace too far gone to
gather up arms,   to save face.
Save what little is left of the *t* in trees
and place.
Roots running down hills.
Hills too high to climb encumbered
with the weight of noise.
Or the sound of bloody jazz in the rain.

Let what we become be who we are.
Be the future. Be the blue guitar.
Be a language that is the dull art of the dead.
Of epiphany up high on shoulders
instead of the head.
And well read.
Reading what only the *o* in poems exclaim.
Calling out numbers.
Calling out names....
Names of prophets that have died
trying to warn daylight of the dark.
The old dog. The new bark.
Echoing from the ridge-tops in flames!

MOOD SWINGS

Press your lips to my face.
Take something fleshless from my cheeks.
Call it the absence of things
or
the dreamed-of absence of fire.

Let the future of autumn know
that this act of love is really only
the death of June.
That the thought of soft cool wind
is the blood that keeps us alive.

When you go down on your knees,
even the Andes shake like a
dove shuddering its wings.
And why do you refer to this as prayer?

Come, raise yourself up from
that beggar's pose.
We've come too far for
old habits and dreams of dirt.
Let's talk about tigers
and
the transfigurative aerodynamics of wings!
These things.
That like uncommon magic,
makes lava out of lightning
lying dormant in our words
and sings!

FAME

Come on, kill me with accolades.
Morphine, that as we speak
burns our names into the black air.
This is a dangerous distance.
Mirrors, jaded as tears,
above my blue bed reflecting only

rocks lined up in rows. Cliffs
like silence spoken by false teeth
falling into the foam of expensive beer.

As if there were hound dogs in our hair, I
am touched by trees.
I wear a hat of ice
to warm my head.
Truth, is like little voices
running through my hands. Snakes
of saffron slicing through
the half of water that is dry.

There is something I can't see
that wants to woo me like a wolf. It is
like an aphrodisiac of blue violets
or
like darkness only looking for a fix.

Once you're on the train and it's moving
you can't get off.
From here, I can see my lover.
Lust falling from her mind like rings—
My arms reach for her like
a creek overflowing its banks with waves.

radiogenesis

When the mica in the sun comes out,
I write brown sentences. Opinions
of the night.
Marrow wanting to preserve itself
like a jar of canned green beans.

In this cold
I am done up in laundry. Cloth
that only resembles clothes.
Products of perilous machines
where we inhale air   into our iron lungs.
Copper flowers that come up in the garden
we left like light years
to come in from the rain.
The flowers are really there.
There is a strong wind.
We can watch them before they blow away.

CENOTAPH

You touch me,
but I am not here.
I am out shopping or
in another century if I am to believe
the words coming from your hands.
When I turn to touch you back
you are there, but busy building walls
and my fingers caress cold rock
of an empty tomb.

AMBITION

Make the angel of God kiss the sacred fire
Open the wild web of worship to the stars
Cover the soul with the blazing music of decay
Speak in flames haunting the passion of perfume
Know why the buddha in the sky was born
    and bring desire to linger in the embrace of warm marble
Surround yourself with familiar flowers
    ferocious to the touch
Question the face of clouds as the flicker
    of cheap candles
Listen to the moon pierce pictures of concrete
    and velvet glass
Remember words that fly or growl wild into
    the open air
Save everything that might remind you of the night
    in loose-fitting clothes
Reek havoc on everything that calls itself truth
    and looks like the end of an affair
Grow great gardens of inedible food from
    seeds flown in from invisible galaxies
Look into the eyes of sadhus for the ration of
    nothingness and the peak of too much sex
Say you are going to meet Lazarus for a pint of beer
    and then steal away to the nearest virgin's tower
Ask nothing of anyone who would ever say no to
    the nature of whether or not reason would be better
    off as the principal of expanded light
Dust off all the evidence of footprints
    of where you have been and
    where you want to go
Be brave and let the scars on your fingers
    grow up and speak for themselves
Tell everyone you know that you are taking a long trip
    and won't be back before twilight
    or the exegesis of morning and a shooting star

SEDUCTION

Dazzle them with blazing voice
Blind them with the flickering dark
Smile and ask roses to blow out candles
   with delicious breath
Free the pink dog from the ghost of oceans
   where the sad girl sings
Beg for sweet pie &
   the aroma of delicious blood
Wake them with needles or smoke
   that haunts the soul
Whisper red secrets that devour drink
   and bring pleasure to the not yet born
Burn blue words like bells crying for God
Kiss them on the breasts like poetry
   as the question of no more night

BRINGING DOWN THE HOUSE

Bring down the universe   from the sky
Make it into a long day
Put evening in the blood of morning
so rain won't blush   and run away
and rivers turn to torrents of fire

Rob peace from time and take it the long way home
Remember the voice of the moon whispering desire
and the trees touching night's dark joy
Hold deep the breath of broken seeds
trusting sleep to heal the stars

Pull petals from the swill of flowers
until not even night will talk to the moon
or moonbeams
Or make promises to the truth in lies
Make heaven scream from the skies
Where there is nothing more to say
or be said   and I go blind begging

For your voice is my sad starlight

AFTER A QUARREL

I know good sex will melt
the stars
and good wine
dazzles the sky
But who am I to
cuddle with angels
or drink champagne from a rich man's ear
Deep in the embrace of reason
sparks flicker to the touch of candles
Whispers shout
blind as bone
And we cover each other with bleeding hair

BLACK BUTTERFLIES

*You ride astride the imaginary in order
to hunt down the real.*
—B. Breytenbach

I have grown accustomed to the curse of chaos.
Words building rhymes and roads that go nowhere.
Like the laughter of low tide
and the roll of slow thunder beneath the black bells.

In the ice-cold granite of where I live
amidst the algebra of anguish and the trigonometry of tears,
many winters have gone by
and there is little left of the sun.
All this time by the water in the hills
you'd think I'd have
at least heard voices or
the spoken wisdom of rocks!
But my life has been like that of a swallow
who mates on an electric wire.
Full of surges and shocks.
Hardly the sage.

Like the stigmata of unused words
it has been here.
Sure as the silver slime of snails
I have felt the trace. Sensed the scent
of something like sex
passing by.

My body was made from the moisture on her mouth.
The blue words slipping out between her lips
redder than strawberries, redder than spice.
When the sleep after sex begins the act of love,
her skin unraveled like badly made twine,
like the flight of birds making footprints in the fog.
Now, like a statue that smiles

radiogenesis

I stand beside her
with svelte liquid drying her green eyes with gold.

She is more than this woman.
She is the time in timelessness that tracks my gray years.
Black butterflies.
The poems her lips have inscribed on my skin.
The offspring of the other, unseen.

All around me the millennial darkness roars.
What has been left   to sever the head of indifference
from its mythical body of grace?
This story of ragas to riches being played out
on the strung-out and broken strings of the poor
is like being run through with the tusks of nothing
but the ivory in fear.

I am here in the shadow of sexless stone.
Building roads that go nowhere.
I am here with the silhouette of words
rounding up strays in the night.
In this chaos I have stumbled onto something
more valuable than painted wings.
It is a chorus of a thousand tone-deaf voices.
And it sings!

WHAT SHE SAID
for Peter Blue Cloud

She said sex is not sacred,
not some hot bleeding kiss
or a ferocious wind on fire, and
believe the breeze when it asks the moon
what to say to the rock crowd of oceans
in a world of small safe ponds.
Believe any drunk, she said, who looks like *haute cuisine*
& has desire or dinner on his mind, and
breathe the smoke of cooked fish and
devour the sweet universe of sugar
while drinking all the nectar that falls from the orbit of Io
or the stars!

WRITING

In the woods of heaven every man in love with ink is

Trying to escape.

Yet, no man runs. Only looks out through trees

Into meadows beyond limbs of greening leaves, hoping

For the form of a woman's body

In a wish of stars....

II.

THE CALLIGRAPHY OF FIRE

The heart is an organ of fire.
—Michael Ondaatje

Just as air, melody is what strikes me most of all in music.
—Gerard Manley Hopkins

MODERN

With eyes now the tongue of language,
the book is buried for all time in
a bed of grass being raised from the dead
in our dreams,
in an age of the dumb and numb of clocks
becoming the digital dogma of waking
in the arms of an electric lover or
a fallen woman without name or face.
With touch-type tempest we
will cry computer-age tears when
the sky falls and the words for help
are forgotten like memory banks buried
forever in history books now only ancient
ice-age ice   cold and frozen solid from
liquid days wondering whether they are
maybe earthbound nights trying to sing in the
key of love longing for the rapture of
simple stillness in the sound of a single
stick against wood or
a splash of ink as
the forgotten longed-for promise of words.

LEARNING LATIN

From the point of no
return I reach for
the moon in the movement of
morning after the radiogenesis
of sleep sleepwalking the
somnambulist floor for hours and
all night when nothing but the
starry-eyed hoot of the owl outside sings
"won't quit you babe" to the beelzebub light
in the street so bright not even the blind
can sleep, can snore loud enough for
summer to know it's spring somewhere when not even
a crocus could care, could call a spade a spade
enamored of lies.
Here, the *hic, haec, hoc, huius, huius, huius*
of the verb *to be* can't even comb its own hair,
can't castrate a noun for the rape of hunger or the forethought
of a hundred bucks barking up the tree of greed going
out of sight into the ozone of oil and the mother of
all wars whenever there is nothing to do but be
homeless under the exegesis of stars and be free.

MIDDLE CLASS

May the love of money become a mask
for our times twiddling its thumbs in the dark
and dreary photosynthesis of sleep
snoring so loud that only a poem could
talk above the roaring silence of sex
making out with the hard-body of handguns
aimed at us all as if we were Indians
and they were a waging war. A war
so willy-nilly it turned infantries to ice
doing the right thing for the wrong reason
that went to the dogs
and the doggerel of mindless talk turning
into fistfights for peace as if the world was
the front row in church
counterfeiting the collection plate in the name of God
and calling it damn, dark, or duty-free rent
like landlords that want to be The King of May
for the price of a gizmo in a garage
that only the neighbor sees and wants
after a day of work becomes a fix beyond
the point of pain
like a bus stopped at the white in our eyes
like light was or would be if it went out and
in darkness all that nothing we learned in school suddenly
came down crashing
on our heads.

THE CALLIGRAPHY OF FIRE

We are neighbors of fire.
—Anne Carson

Where the warm-blooded fish is mad with
the moon in the man talking in tongues I
sit amidst dowsing darkness   tired of rain.
Knee-deep in the mud of love like a man who
washes windows with the tears of a bell, near the
high-heeled trees, near commitment to the
knifeblade of a kiss, the searing heat of the word "sweetheart"
makes love to the tongue that brought an end to talk
wagging like the blasphemy of the color blue in
a lost weekend of dreams.
Voiceless, my pricked fingers bleeding ink
dance across what were once bridges
now only the white mud in the thunder of silence
playing bingo with balls, playing
preludes of a Mardi Gras ghost on the
wavelike pipeline of pain moving toward sand like
the chambered nautilus in a Chinese book.
Here where the wallow of fame flooded from the lack of light
makes moonshine make me look like a confessed criminal, like
the sun stealing the rings of Saturn from space, I
kneel to nothing   not even the knees of the she-god king
stroking my sleep   like brushstrokes over the flames of an
open fire and the sounds of midnight   like morning
singing *Hail-Marys* in the rain....

FROZEN MUSIC
for Joy Harjo

Never was the never in nearsighted closer to
this heart of rain seeking the storm. Dark clouds of brilliance
rubbing the back of these hills. How hallowed ground
has grown again into the hallways of sacred space.
Only love could have given this tongue a song. Sheer jazz
from a jew's harp of trees tricked by wind. Tricked
and trapped in the riddle of my name. Hidden in
the implicate order of space. After eons. Behind the
hologram of race.
The better the story the bigger the bang.
And the loud noise of the fire asleep slides off into
the silence of unknown sound. Sacrilege to the thought of
summer lusting after the memory of sex with spring.
Lips discovering the trade-routes of thighs. Hands holding hills
of snowflesh more hallowed than the holy grail.
Given is what is gotten back. A frozen music.
A jazz in love with the isn't of ice. The kiss of death. Of spice!
Beyond the bare-breasted moon and bimbos of the Milky Way,
Beethoven records his first hit. In the night below zero
with a wind-chill of a million to one. Rough odds
going against the snake-eyes of war. The boxcars of space.
Or the fugue of a frigid bride.
Never was the upbeat genesis of fame so close to cash. Like
trying to get a grant from God. A farm for a few farthings.
Or the world in a card game of empty bucks.
Beyond where the gray rain of birds train for miles across mountains
of smoky grace, is pigment of painted place. Landscapes frozen in
acrylic time feeding on the afterthought of nails
pounding like angry waves, like lost loves in a lifetime,
against the apocalyptic shore.

ORACLE

Once we had asked the question as to the source of daylight,
the shutters of the self and the sashes of the soul flew open
and even the glass that was wept into windows to hide the pain
blew out like a blue breeze before the disbelief in my eyes
that ran from my head like a scared child that had never seen
the sun running like this from the light that no longer lived
in a box or a brothel but began begging to be told the truth
now that heaven had slid off its pedestal of prayer to come
down to earth and memory of the birth of ignorance from all
that longing through safe passage   or fields of rain.

SOMEBODY

I live in a land
where somebody made love to somebody
who sang softly to the heart of
somebody, who got up and turned on
the light for somebody, who
played music the next day for somebody
who loved music more than life, and died listening to Bach
with somebody at the same time that the
wailing wall fell down from the weight
of too many hands, hands of too many somebodys
broke the camel's back which was bought
by somebody in the business of fixing back
what was wrong with some country's leaders
and the land he loved during a
time of peace when no peace came-and-went without
so much as a thank you or a show of hands
for somebody trying to write the wrong of
revolutions gone mad, mad at somebody born
in a church that belongs to somebody who wears ten
golden rings, who gave grace to somebody
who didn't even grieve, who lived in a far-away
land of things, things without wings, with somebody
she didn't even know, who was her mirror of
not-knowing that she looked into and saw
somebody else we'd never known who wanted to
run off with somebody to Corfu or Crete where they
could drink wine made of dates with somebody that
at night would read to them of the future of forbidden wars
which were no longer fought with somebody who showed up
to fight but was at home in the woods with somebody
making love.

MYTHOLOGY

What web would pierce windows &
a free heart shining hotter than sun,
softer than blood could cry
were it cut from morning with a whisper &
water was perfume of warm rain on
sad laughing animals &
an ocean blushed with green breezes
that kiss color & the cup of fire
when wind takes the world prisoner &
the work of poison breathes song into dirt,
puts voice in a land that sings &
in singing gently flies away....

SOUR CANDY

As sure as the bees return for the thousandth time
to water, the wind
will wash the hair of sunlight
wanting to comb rust (as if it were youth
trying to break banks and the habits of old dreams)
into the neatly groomed locks of age
and the street-hawking twilight
comes door to door selling winter as what would be sour candy
to one who sits in the lamplight
of a far-woods tower   falling deeper   like pen and ink,
into a pile of poems.

radiogenesis

WHEN THE WHITE LIGHT
FROM THE LAMP TURNED ON

When the white light from the lamp turned on in the tower
and the way we look at the moon came down and sat
beside our bed, where was the *no* in noon or the
might in midnight in the dark of a room where no hair
could hide, no time could bide, no sea could tide....
nor could we be better than bare-breasted in our suits
of rags, rags richer than white was when it was black
or what red was when the ten thousand words I know showed
up in a sack of silence to tell me something about love.

When the silly teeth in this tower fall from the roof of
the mouth of the moon, and what was light from a window
becomes a mirror moving through the screen door of a dream,
you can call to me from everywhere but Egypt and ask the
time of day, or the way to the nearest pub put back on
the map of the edge of a stool where we sit all night
waiting for some she-gone ghost to come through the door and
then strip down to the toes to make sure we are really
there before asking us for a drink and a ride home.

WITH DEEP BREEZE SLOW ON AIR

*God's great power is in the gentle breeze,
not in the storm.*
— Tagore

With deep breeze slow on air
& smoke in blue grass
haunting the sky & beating words
with red music
deep in the neck & never dead
your sex blushes
like old art   warm as the word *antique*
free as fire kissing the glass in God
where windows were &
skin felt pale as petals
born singing but not sacred
& soaking the wave-wild night
where water was darker than midnight &
born of dirt
blushing like girls
high on sweet smoke
blowing color like cold kisses to be put
on as the skin of snakes would come off of hands
like gloves
fresh as flowers & then use the
scent for warmth   as spice

LONG LINES
after Bachelard
for Sam Gray

Again, the teeth of night have wandered into the room of sleepless sleep, like politicians drowning in the wake of their own dreams.
Here behind walls with a roof built like prison guards to protect my muse, where woodstove burns words not wood from mysterious heat, where everything moves as if it were a prerequisite to God, the fire grows and even grins in the face of my longing for the absence of ice.

WILL THE NIGHT EVER REMEMBER ITS DREAMS?

Drugged on cash, the politicians are dreaming of dolphins who breathe water as if it were air. Air that sees the nothing in the all of eyelids still hiding sleep like glasses are the porches of the eyes that have found, in place, the memory of silence still resting there like a chair rocking in the sad wind.

KNOWLEDGE

Soon as the sugar drains off from the dead
the dead will be braver than what was brave.
Will be left to grow old a groan after what was
sex before ice broke loose from the heat
of passion playing tricks on the eyes of oasis
he thought was Love lingering down where
he used to drink all night to forget
even the forgetting he fought for and lost
like the runaway of would-be wives disappearing
in the shadow of midnight looking for light.
"*Ho*" was all he said when what might have been
the wind kept calling his name. Calling his name
like street-signs whispering around the
sins of roads like they were poems. Hollering
"*hidey-ho*" half a life longer than
any fool would watch while waiting
for a bus that came, went, and came
and went again all in the time the iris in
an eye could blink before being blinded
by the night. How could he have known?
Answers were only afterthoughts of the shock of sex.
Something moaning with bones.
Where men were only women dancing
on the black side of glass.
Being picked over after wine had already been made
and waiting in buckets of old wood
like poets   for the promise of a rush of stars!

ESTATES

And who will be the slave that drives
the slaver to drink or be drunk on his own wine,
that tips the end of one life over to meet the
other like spilt blood or a serf
with nothing to eat? O why O why
must those who sweat blood and work for those
shy of blisters make love to only
the sharp end of coins? Money
that won't even cut into the price of meat.
Happy are they who share. Giving
what was equal to their own weight in love.
While owners feed forgetfulness
with their exotic wines.
Writing checks in the blind ink of avarice
while those who work beg for nothing
more than a promise of a prayer or
a wish for all those broken dreams.

Biltmore Winery
Asheville, NC
December 12, 1987

radiogenesis

ON A WEE WHITE ROCK

I sit on a wee white rock where the sky
melts the mist of my muse and I
write my first words on this plaid land
larger than life that has lingered like the
high pitch of pipes in my heart or the
songs of MacLean that bring tears to
my eyes now open to the lushness of all this green.
Green that even a gray day lies to,
doing its best to defeat the heart that
needs to be here in this high land
that leans on the sea like a crofter
leans late at night on the bar with
his pint of ale after all day digging
peat from the black bottoms where the
last tears of snow have stopped running from
winter and the death of blue sky and
daylight gone to the latitude of a tilted earth,
where there is little left in the heart
of worth, when dying seems the better part
of birth, I sit up on my wee white rock
and rage at the crofter's right
to be poor, to be land rich,
richer than landed gentry
and lords or pious monks
building bridges to take history away
from the land now taken by tourists
and greedy cars that can't think
for themselves or know
where the road will go...go on rolling
like round rocks roll like dice
or a pound and
what a pound can buy to try and bring back
love to this land that has left
and gone to the cities in banks to be

radiogenesis

bet on when the horses run or what is
left of the light when the light is
gone from the farms, fields and skye
and taken in tour boats
to the National Bank where there used to be
grazing sheep
that once upon a time was a wee glen
where children saw faeries
and old men snored under the weeping vines.

Isle of Skye, Scotland
July 8, 1995

radiogenesis

BY WHITE ROAD AND THISTLE

By Oppressions woes and pains
By your sons in servile chains
We will drain our dearest veins
But they shall be free!
    —Robert Burns
     from "Scots Whn' hae"

By white road and thistle
I raise up my pen and write
against the roar of silence in
the green hills of Glenfinnan
that look more like mountains than the moors
of the mainland that have taken roots
away from the flowers in farms
and the old ways water used to
sing in the mouths of deer come down
to drink from the trains that
bring history from the sky like
the single malt in rain
in a fine sideways slant
of mist that only the midges or
those lost at sea would drink
trying to find their way back home
from the flood of blood in wars
waged in the name of clans
or the love of the queen's
face on a silver pound
like the other word for greed
when all along we knew
it was the makar and the mountains that we need.

     Glenfinnan, Scotland
     1995

radiogenesis

VOICE
for Maura O'Connell

From the clouds in County Clare,
from the burren branch,
from bard William's pen
broken and daft of wind and rain
where small flowers grow in the cracks
of endless stone only a stone's throw from the tor—
that voice
like a bell lodged in a heron's neck
that not only rings but sings,
sings swash-buckled songs that only
the *p* in pirate could steal
from the King of Hearts or
the prince of whales holding forth
a league beneath the surface of wet salt
that washes her brow with
a ring of curls in the hot lights
with high notes that go right
through the roof, go right on
singing only the best song ever scribbled
or sung then signed in blood
red as her Irish cheeks burned from wind
from the west blowing a gale that
when it comes from those lips wants
to be kissed by a major key and
maybe even a man who would be willing
to lose his mind and heart to
the quiet in a hurricane that has taken
a breath before the next verse and is working its way
back home.

County Clare, Ireland
1995

radiogenesis

NEWGRANGE

When I walked into the ancient room of stone
with only the light from a match,
when the light went out
I was more alone than
even the fear of dark—
which was everywhere
and nowhere,
which is where I was.
In there. Wombed.
Outside   of even my own body.
Back in time. Yet timeless.
Blind. Eyes imagining
how things end.
Until   the first rays of the sun
shone in the passageway,
and then into the central chamber
where I found I was sitting on
an altar   as if a sacrifice
for the light as it reflected off
mirrors made of mica
set in concave stones
to a single point on the ceiling.
Becoming a new year.

County Meath, Ireland
1995

THE WILD DUCKS AT COOLE
for Nan

Where the wild ducks at Coole
wade and quack in the river for a
grab of green grass growing
near the brown rocks
covered with moss and the
history of walls is
where we have come to
honor trees
by carving our names with knives
in gardens for those who come from Ballylee
and towers where swords of samurai float in
the air of rooms ruined by love
and through woods and on paths
for walking where we,
like howling horsemen, pass by and
are here to see swans
that are only here in autumn
wild as these ducks or
how I see you   nonethnic but
as white as the wind in your hair.

Coole Park
County Galway, Ireland
1995

EVENSONG
for Bobi Jones
after Gerard Manley Hopkins

Even the evening's song sings
a cappella after all
the lips have closed
and silence sounds like so much
breeze empty between branches
of old trees
too tired to fight the air or
any ambush of guns gunning down
children, churchmen, or common thieves.
Will a round of ammo give our nightmares
wings? Will things?
Even the aftermath of nouns
won't give verbs their rights to sing,
to hold high *C* in their hand and say
"I am"
or
"I am not alone in this night."
Night that no longer leads to daylight
or out of darkness deader than
doornails
that do the job on anyone that
wants in
or wants in on the deal of
high priests and kings
cornering the market on the flim-flam
of finance and flicks.
No, not even the *aber* in Aberystwyth
will turn its head the other way
will say *bont* in place of the word *bre*
or that singing is a song
or something sung to give way to
the wind,

radiogenesis

the wind wanting to know the why, when, and where of
a fortune that would leave a farmhouse in ruin
or runes in a heap of rust
rotting like a first language
or life
absent of machines.
Even the *n* in nod has
gone to sleep
so that soldiers can sneak up and
kill the queen of hearts
before she has sex with a bee
and brings fiction down from the skies
again
and the end of love
that left its lover
in a bed of tears turned down
like the tide in a tourniquet
pulled too tight
to hold water in
a bowl of lies as leverage for the leaving,
the heartbreak,
or what dies.

Aberystwyth, Wales
November, 1997

radiogenesis

THE FLORESCENT EYE
 for N.

Netherworlds are the nothing of something gone
and you are the sum of things to come.
Tell the beggar and the thief that dawn is really
all that's left of love and watch how they dance
in vain to where I already am and where
every eye in the room is on you lit up like
Saturn showing stars the way to the hub of
essence becoming silver quicker than the eye blinks and
yesterday I will come to you with bad mood bells on
to your door even when you're gone
or giving recitals to the wind in Wales
or wonderland lit up like lasers in
your eyes.

Laugharne, Wales
1993

radiogenesis

THE BIG HERE
THE LONG NOW

The singing and the song not sung
sits still in me. Sits still where
even the dead can dance. Where
even my heart has died from
terrible miracles manifest in streets
and designer plagues in the history of the
LONG NOW hiding in a parallel universe of sleep.
Birds. What birds? What song did you sing
back then before the promise of another day
or night alone in the **BIG HERE** or there
you'll never see? See singing. Singing like
only birds can sing beneath the clavichord sky,
in the invisible trees, in a chant of air,
in your silk-auburn hair that hides my eyes, hides
my hearing for the radiogenesis of dreams that are the
aurora borealis of bed and bedtime tales
printed on the pages of your thighs like
the miracle of two hills
hidden from town, hidden from skies
of **THE BIG HERE, THE LONG NOW:**
the short step between being born, waiting to die,
dancing with the dead or the dog at the door in the name
of God or the damned rich begging for lies.
Birds. Brown hair. A black song from the
abracadabra of buildings born because we
have no past. No part-time love for what
ticks and tocks. What talks to each other
in song. In the sounds only the lonely hear
at night in their beds, speaking in tongues.
I have heard the deaf and dumb of the dream.
The ambient sunrise coming from a
board of keys. The beat of inaudible air. Articulate
down to the last dime. The last rhyme.

Thomas Rain Crowe

radiogenesis

Dash of sweet salt in the wound.
Wounded and wanting your veil of hair.
THE BIG HERE. THE LONG NOW.
The pachelbel of memory, the liszt of sleep.
Dug deep.
Deeper than sleep-burnt beggars and bums
that are giddy and grateful for the *r* in rest.
The *t* in guitar. Or the *c* in what
still can dance. To the beat of ***THE BIG HERE.***
The song of ***THE LONG NOW.*** Warp speed in silence.
Gift-wrapped in violence. Under clavichord skies.
In invisible trees. In the chant of air.
In your silk-auburn hair. In your eyes.

IO

Somewhere in the smoke-alarm of the night, Io
is tucking Jupiter into bed. The way the full moon
is blinded by the blanket of Earth when light and darkness
bring out their rondelet of aching orb-like limbs
and do the bony contra-dance of dreams.

In the womb of the Milky Way
sperm is the fly-by full moon making a pass
at the snatch of Earth.
Tracing the wet shadow of a would-be pen across
white skin, whiter than night
and the wannabe of poems.
Poems singing to the open grave of innocence
inoculated with the warm wind coming
from the starburst epiphany of black holes
blinded by sight that seeing, says:
"Take off the old dark coat and
put on the smoking moonbeam's cosmic cape of light!"

MACHU PICCHU

When morning
is
also
the night
in red shadow
on
squares
of perfect stone
fit by ghost-hands
the lost city
appears
where
watchman's shack
catches first glimpse
of
solstice sun
and condor-
like
a puma
prowls near
Inti Huatana
in clouds
where the sun is hitched
to music of pan pipes
and
tight-fitting stones
in step terraces
where *alpaca* graze
beneath
Torreon door:
an altar rock
glistens
in a rush of light.

Urubamba Valley, Peru
2004

radiogenesis

WHAT WOULD THE WOULD-BE WISE

What would the would-be wise be
if *to be* was what we have already become?
Have bought and paid for in lies. Have
hung up on our walls to dry—
What would the pious or the pretty think
if the price for proof went up like the
yeast in bread? Went down like a whore
for the glitter in the grasp of a drunk.
O you would-be wise, take all the indigo in ink and drink!
And like all the hemlock in hell, become ice.

Where there are mountains being born from the blue of sky
or valleys rising from the four-letter words of space,
destiny loads the train of years with mirrors and the
quicksilver of ancient glass.
So what would the would-be wise be
when the shortest distance between two points is
no longer a line? No longer the lineage of leisure or
new green ink. A little less anxious I think.
And in the moonlight, like ancient knowledge still
the same, the poet stares into candleflame.

THE ALMA MATER OF A KISS
for C.L.

Only the alma mater of space will wait for
what's going down in the deltas of human life and
the inlets of what was once Mars and now is
the bar-room brawl of belief that smothers our
dreams dreaming of what the sex of salvation is
about to become any instant as the orbiting aura
of Earth is turning black in the absence of light
which I see in your eyes as eyeless and almost
like rain would be if I were apples and
needed to grow, go, gorge myself on the photo-
synthesis of your skin seeking itself in what's
left of me or to the right of politics reaching
into the cookie-jar of your soul for sugar and
pulling out instead   my kiss.

IMMORTALITY

When I write on your white skin with
dark ink and the calligraphy of unspoken vowels
covers arms and legs   page-like,
covers back, belly and thighs
and the thought that is born from words
makes midnight blink and the morning go blind,
I find the wherewithall to
make my mistakes   indelible
and
stained in truth so that
they will last   even after
your body has gone to the morgue
and only ashes remain
on stretched canvas
as a work of art.

NOT EVEN IN THE NIL OF NIGHT

Not even in the nil of night
does the door-knocking silence
seem so loud as
when you call my name
like the ghost of a blackbird from lips
only open to the kiss of air
entering my sleep so sound
that there are dreams drawing
up to the edge of morning not even
the sun could see   so far away
it is that I have spent
my life waiting for light from
the first moment I saw her
there running
away from the waves
farther and farther toward only
a line of sky leaving
the memory of feet in the sand where
maybe somewhere she is and
is waiting   out-of-breath and
understands the cosmiconsciousness of morning and
wherever she is
I am.

radiogenesis

WHERE THE WHITE WAVES

Where the white waves
wear away the sand and
land is where I rest my feet
swaggering along the warm and
quiet shore   talking to gulls
and pelican pulling the
erudite air along in the
beak-biffing foam of waves where
no man is or fish are
in eyes so old that not even the
aurora borealis of sound could hear
the sea-sqawking song now
not even coming from all that noise
not counting the million
grains of sand in one square inch
of a thought there
inside the dark of a crab hole
I look in
to wonder what
is there amongst the lack of
sea oats and
find you.

Thomas Rain Crowe

MEETINGS

What if words or we were
star-crossed and   afraid of the night.
Night lit with the way the moon mirrors
the caress of inner speech. Or
how the crossroads make love to
the echo of reflected light.
Wouldn't the wonder of winter freeze
if by chance our bodies should meet?
Should speak   and become then the apparition of ice—
Only the *escra* or
the excelsior of this thought can dance,
can do *can-can* on the grave of Death and
not die.
Here Hiroshima is
blowing kisses to the wind. To
the marriage of how next we will meet.
Like two eyes searching for
the scent of what the other has said. One the bleeder
and the other the one that has bled.
One the moonlight and
the other the foot of the bed.

About the Author

Thomas Rain Crowe is an internationally recognized poet and translator whose work has been published in several languages. He is the author of twenty books of original works, translations, anthologies and recordings including *The Laugharne Poems,* written at the Dylan Thomas home in Laugharne, Wales and published by Welsh publisher Gwasg Carreg Gwalch; *Thomas Rain Crowe & The Boatrockers LIVE,* which received praise from poet-musician Joy Harjo and Pete Townshend of The Who; and the multi-award-winning book of nonfiction *Zoro's Field: My Life in the Appalachian Woods,* published in 2005 by the University of Georgia Press. As an editor, he has been an instrumental force behind such magazines as *Beatitude, Katuah Journal* and the *Asheville Poetry Review.* As a translator, he has translated collections by poets including Hafiz and Yvan Goll. His archives have been purchased and are collected by the Duke University Special Collections Library. He lives in the Smoky Mountains of rural western North Carolina.

Photo by Kenn Long

Other titles by *THOMAS RAIN CROWE*

POETRY

Learning To Dance
Poems For Che Guevara's Dream
Deep Language
The Personified Street
New Native
Water From The Moon
The Laugharne Poems
Poems From Zoro's Field
The Book of Rocks

TRANSLATIONS

Why I Am A Monster (Hughes-Alain Dal)
In Wineseller's Street: Renderings of Hafiz
Drunk on the Wine of the Beloved: 100 Poems of Hafiz
10,000 Dawns: Love Poems of Yvan & Claire Goll
Pourquoi Je Suis Une Monstre (Hughes-Alain Dal)
The Dead Lips Dance (Hughes-Alain Dal)

ANTHOLOGIES

Writing The Wind: A Celtic Resurgence (The New Celtic Poetry)
10 Great Neglected Poets of the 20th Century
The Baby Beats & The 2nd San Francisco Renaissance

RECORDINGS

The Sound of Light
Live at the Green Door